Other Books

by

Nancy Kuykendall

Nonfiction

Mornings on the Porch

Ordinary Wonders

Our Daily Moments

Now I Lay Me Down TO SLEEP-

Help and Hope for the Sleepless

God Is Not Silent -

One Woman's Encounters with God

Fiction

The Old Woman - Book One - Meet Rose

The Old Woman – Book Two – A New Year

The Old Woman – Book Three – A Time of Change

BEFORE GOD WITH AN OPEN HEART

Daily Prayers

NANCY KUYKENDALL

Before God with an Open Heart

Daily Prayers

by

Nancy Kuykendall

Printed in the United States

Visit the author's website www.nancykuykendall.com

Cover Photo: iStock image

Cover Design and Formatting: Waqar Nadeem

ACKNOWLEDGEMENTS

I wrote this book quietly, since the text within are personal prayers now shared.

My editor has been involved in this project. I'd like to thank, **author M. A. Street** once again, for his diligence in editing my manuscript. Mike never seeks to change my words, intent, or voice. He graciously helps me write my best to express my thoughts as well as possible. I appreciate you, Mike, and I absolutely know God sent you to me.

My husband, **Steve**— my closest friend, biggest fan, and cheerleader. His understanding of my passion to write and his encouragement that I continue is priceless. Thank you, Steve. I cherish you. You are a gift from God.

Praise be to **Almighty God** for his many blessings and graciousness toward me.

Amen

Nancy

PREFACE

I felt a conviction and desire to write, and share, these prayers. Private prayers seem an odd thing to share publicly, yet this isn't the first book of its kind. I was originally inspired to write this type of book after reading John Baillie's, A Diary of Private Prayer, first published in 1949. It's a classic. It was written in a more formal manner than this book. I wrote exactly how I talk to God, which is quite informal. These are simple prayers, in simple language.

The prayers within this book are shared to express the thoughts, wishes, questions, and vulnerability of all humans. We are alike, you and me. We share the same joys, fears, sorrows, experiences, and we have the same Creator God. We live in the same world—for all its good and bad.

These prayers contain many of my talks with God. I write with a myriad of emotions including gratitude, fear, anger, sorrow, confusion, joy, thanksgiving, and more. I ask God questions. I deal with God's reprimands and teaching. I seek his leading and his plans for my life. I praise him.

Sometimes I pray simply asking God to speak to me. On the days I hear God speak, I am elated. When days go by that I don't hear him, I seek after him more diligently. I yearn to hear God's voice.

It is my hope that these prayers will resonate with you, and you won't feel alone. We're on this earthly journey together and we are never alone. God is beside us every step of the way if we allow him.

If you're not in the habit of praying daily, reading a prayer a day may help you build the habit.

May God richly bless you,

Nancy

"Then you will call on me and come and pray to me,

and I will listen to you."

(Jeremiah 29:12 NIV)

Day 1

Good morning, God.

I'm awake and am aware of your presence. I'm alive to see a new day, and I know it's a gift from you. I know too, Lord, that if I'm here you must have a plan for me on this day. What's this day about?

I lie snug in my bed, comfortable and warm. I'm grateful. I'm aware that many across the world are sleeping on dirt floors in far less comfort than I enjoy. I don't take my comfort for granted, Lord. Thank you for my soft, warm, comfortable bed.

I hear the robins outside in the elm tree singing their cheery song. I like the robins. Maybe it's their song. Maybe it's because of the pair I watched care for their baby—that fledgling in our yard a few years ago. I even fed that baby a worm. Remember God? That was a special moment. The morning I discovered that little bird asleep on our driveway, I bent down to pet him. Remember that? He startled and opened his eyes to stare at me, but he didn't budge. He let me touch him and talk to him. I thank you for those experiences. I know you were behind them, letting me interact with a bird in such ways.

It's time I get up. This morning is starting very peacefully, God. Thank you. I know that by the end of the day much could have changed. We never know our future, but I feel safe and content right now. In peace or in trouble, I know I need only call your name and you will come to me.

Let me hear your voice today, God. I yearn to hear you speak.

Amen

Day 2

God,

Thank you for the unexpected encouragement today. You know I sometimes struggle through the days wondering if any of my efforts have value. Just when I want to give up, you send an encouraging word from somewhere. Thank you for your faithfulness to me.

I take my work and the calling you've given me seriously, yet at times it seems it only matters to me and to you. There's a feeling I get of being alone, on a deserted island, speaking into the wind that blows my words away to nowhere. Just when I believe my work doesn't matter, you send encouragement that lifts my spirit and lets me know I'm doing okay and should keep on—that you use my words for your purposes when you see fit, whether I'm aware of it or not. I know if I do my part, if I do what you ask, you will use it, in your way and in your timing and for your glory, God.

Be with those today who are struggling with discouragement. Life can be lonely. Send them a word that spurs them on, just as you have done for me. Help us always see our value from your viewpoint, no other. It is you, Lord, who gives us our value.

Amen

Day 3

What a beautiful morning, God.

As I sit in my special area in the backyard and view your creation, I am filled with peace. The sunrise brings hope for the new day. With you, Lord, there is always hope. Thank you for this new day.

Watching the trees, now leafed out in their summer glory swaying in the breeze, as I too feel the breeze against my skin and through my hair. I feel a calming caress from you, Lord. The trees offer themselves to other life so generously. The birds and squirrels make their nests in the trees and the tree shades the yard for our comfort. They are beautiful. I feel they have a consciousness, an awareness of some kind, and I talk to them, Lord. I admire your trees.

The birds and animals in the yard, Lord. They bring entertainment and the simple enjoyment of watching life. The birds sing and fly and eat from the feeders I fill for them. They chatter amongst themselves. The tree squirrels make me laugh with their silly antics in play and in nibbling the food I've left for them. They are energetic and cute. The ground squirrels too, God. They are busy right now and I watch them run in the field and into our yard, as they come to enjoy the seed I've thrown in the grass. The rabbits, Lord, so quiet and gentle, munching the greens and flowers and seeds that sustain them, stretching out to lie in the cool grass, or playing leapfrog with each other. The new baby bunnies are a joy to see. The chipmunk who slinks through the grass coyly catches my attention as he meanders by. The menagerie of life in the yard is a blessing.

Lord, thank you for the trees, and flowers, and the creatures, and for the joy they bring.

Amen

Day 4

Dear God,

Please forgive me. I am feeling impatient with people. I don't understand why so many choose to continue to suffer and struggle rather than turn to you. We all do this sometimes, Lord, but I know I can run to you in times of trouble, and you will be there. When I seek you, you draw near to me. It's a truth I've experienced over and over. Why, Lord, do so many people choose to suffer rather than seek your help? If they would only test your promises, they would find you are faithful. They would find help.

I know, Lord God, that we will all face struggles in this world. I know we will sometimes suffer even when we call on you, but your loving kindness and faithfulness make it bearable, Lord. You are our sustainer. You quiet our anxiety. You give us peace and joy even in our trials and pain. Lord, you give us strength to endure and carry on.

Above all, Lord God, you give us hope for a better tomorrow. You give us hope in the eternity we will spend with you when we leave this earth. Earthly death comes to all, Lord. But in the salvation you grant when we reconcile with you, you give us eternal life. Eternity, with you Almighty God, free from the woes of this earthly existence.

I pray, Father, that I will always remember that you are the source of my strength. I pray all will turn to you, truly know you, have a relationship with you, discover your peace and strength and find the joy that passes understanding in life now and eternal.

Grant me patience as I deal with myself and others.

Amen

Day 5

Hello God. It's me again.

I'm still questioning people. Help me understand others and myself. We cannot see as clearly as you do.

Lord, does it make sense that a person who professes to know you will never speak your name, will never talk of their relationship with you, will never speak of prayer? Does it make sense that a person who knows you will call upon the universe and ask for positive thoughts, rather than call upon you in prayer? You made the universe! We should call upon you.

Lord God Almighty, can a person truly know you and not talk about you and speak your name? You have told us to shine our light, to tell others of you, to pray to you—talk to you. If a person truly knows you, wouldn't they do these things? How could they stay silent?

Lord, we are not to judge each other, but sometimes what one says and does, or doesn't do, does not seem to prove having a relationship with you. I know some of us are quieter than others, some more shy and inhibited. But, God, how can one stay silent when they know you and have experienced you? Once a person knows you, they can never be the same. We are changed when we know you. How can one not find boldness enough to speak of you? It seems inconsistent, God. All nature seems to sing your praises. I want to sing your praises. I cannot stay silent about you Almighty God. How can one who claims to know you keep silent?

Lord, I ask that all of us who know you will be bold and speak your name and praise your name. If anyone falsely believes he or she knows you, please speak to them and show yourself to them, so he or she can come to know you in all truth.

Lord God, I know you. You know me. Correct me when I am wrong. Help me speak boldly of you. I will praise your name.

Amen

Day 6

Lord, I need you.

I received bad news today. I'm reaching the age when health issues can occur, large and small. It's hard for me to accept any possible problem because I've always enjoyed excellent health. In a way, I'm spoiled, Lord. I've run free, slept well, breathed easily, moved easily, and had strength. I've enjoyed sound body and mind. But, Lord, our bodies grow old little by little and become frail.

I don't feel old, Lord. Yes, my hair is graying, some joints are stiff with arthritis, I'm not as firm or strong and small pains plague me. Now, Father God, I have a frailty to think about. It will remind me I am no longer young, even if I don't feel old or think of myself as old. There is no stopping a body from growing older. Little by little we decay. Our earthly bodies won't last forever. I know this.

Lord God, help me accept my aging body. Allow me the grace to grow old without complaint and to embrace each day. I desire to grow old gracefully and with dignity. I want to grow wiser as I grow older. I want to be a good example to younger women, or even women my age struggling to accept the changes that come with old age.

God, I thank you for every day of health I've enjoyed and will enjoy. I ask for patience with myself as my body loses strength and vigor. I ask that you help me be the best I can be at every age and every day of life you give me. I ask that you give me courage in any illness or old age frailties that may come my way.

I know, Lord, that earthly life and earthly bodies fade away, but you have something better waiting for me in your heavenly kingdom.

Amen

Day 7

Father,

I feel renewed today. Thank you for hearing my prayers, calming me, and giving me another good night of sleep. Sleep is healing. Thank you for the peaceful morning. Thank you for the opportunity and joy in writing these prayers for this book I long to share.

Lord, not everyone is having a peaceful day. One quick look at the news or social media and despair everywhere is evident. There is no end to the depravity of man and the depression so many live with daily. Struggling to get through each day is the theme of so many lives. Life has dealt a very tough hand to many people. Others bring on their difficulties day after day, stuck in a vicious cycle of negativity and poor choices.

Lord God, have compassion on us. We are far removed from the ideal you first had planned for mankind. For those who don't know you, everyday must be a heavy and difficult road. For those who do know you, we also struggle but not without your help and hope. Your hand in our lives makes all the difference in being able to live joyfully.

Lord God, forgive us, have pity on us, show us your compassion, guide us, and help us.

I seek you, Lord, and you come to me. Thank you.

Amen

Day 8

Lord,

Some decisions can be difficult to make. Some choices are crystal clear, while some are thick as mud…the answer impossible to find. I'm in one of those "thick as mud" times, Lord. Frankly, I think I know what I want, but I don't know what *you* want. I need to know what you want in this matter. What do you expect from me? Please God, make it clear.

I know decisions can often be undone, but I want to know before I decide if I'm following my own selfish way, or if you are truly leading me to a new path to end a long-held vocation. Is it time to let it go and focus more fully elsewhere?

I need your guidance, Lord. Is this a job I should do until death, or is it time to let it go and let others takeover? I can think it through both ways, yet not reach a concrete answer.

Maybe there isn't a concrete answer. Maybe it's okay whichever way I choose.

As I said, Lord, it's clear as mud. Please help me know your will and the answer.

Amen

Day 9

Heavenly Father,

I'm perplexed. How can two people with the exact same information arrive at two very different conclusions? It seems everything is divided. Even among those of like faith and beliefs opposite conclusions are drawn. How can that be, Lord? If followers of you don't agree, then how can we know what is right and true? You'd think we'd draw the same conclusions—conclusions coming from your teachings.

This world is confusing, Lord. It truly is. I read your words in the Bible and take them for truth but am I understanding the truth? My fellow believers draw different truths from your word. God, there is only one truth. Your truth.

You gave us commandments, Lord. Commandments we all too often break. Not only that, but we also interpret them differently. How can we derive two meanings from the simple words, "Thou shalt not murder" or "Thou shalt not steal"? It makes no sense. Are there really varying levels or categories of right and wrong? I cannot see that, God. The laws seem clear to me, even if we do sometimes break them.

None of us are without sin, Lord. I understand we have weaknesses and flaws. Yet can we not know your divine truth, the one truth? Help me know your absolute truth, Father God.

Amen

Day 10

Father,

Thank you for meaningful friendships. I am blessed to have special and wonderful friends—friends I can openly talk to and confide in. I'm grateful for these friends, Lord. Thank you for bringing them into my life, especially when I was seeking someone in my own town to connect with and spend time with. Thank you for that special friend, God.

I wished for and then prayed earnestly for a local friend. I remember the day you brought that person to mind. I was so happy when she said she was also interested in a friendship. I enjoy our time together. Thank you for her.

God, thank you, too, for my far away friends—those I know in person and for a special pen pal friend whom I know only through letters, text, written emails, and audio emails. We've never met but she has become a dear friend. This is such a special gift, Lord. There are others who are dear to me, Lord, whom I've never met in person.

These special friends, those I have met face to face and those I have not, are very dear to me, Father. Truly there are friends who are as close as sisters. They are gifts from you, Lord.

Thank you.

Amen

Day 11

Father God,

Today is a holiday in our country. It's Independence Day for the United States. People are off work; many businesses are closed. The day has been quiet and peaceful but tonight the sky will be filled with the sights and sounds of fireworks. Our town and our entire country will celebrate our independence.

While some are celebrating our great land, others are lamenting what it has become. It seems year after year, decade after decade, our country becomes fraught with bigger problems and more angst. But, Lord, since the beginning of time there have been tremendous troubles and all sorts of evil. The evils of today aren't so new, yet they feel heavy and burdensome, and even frightening, Lord.

The world is more complicated than it used to be, and there is so much more in front of our eyes and ears every day. We are overwhelmed, God.

Help me remember to pray for this great country, Lord. To us it feels like a mess, but I know from listening to those from other cultures who now live here, that they consider life to be much better in the United States than other places. How is it that immigrants so speak highly of the U.S.A. while we who were born and raised here often see only the negative in our society.

Lord, there is much wrong in our country but let us be grateful for the bounties, freedom, and opportunities we can have here that don't exist in other lands. May we count our blessings. May we remember to pray for our leaders no matter how we feel about them. Those who don't know you need prayer most. May we pray for and raise up our country to acknowledge you, God.

Amen

Day 12

Hello God,

Today I'm aware of many friends and family and strangers who are grieving the loss of a loved one. They are drowning in sorrow. Lord God, please help those who are mourning. Please lighten their grief. Let them have restful sleep, Lord. Let their sleep give them a break from their emotional pain. Lord, help them breathe—some can barely catch their breath. Help each find the strength for every new day to live on without their loved one.

Father God, I especially pray for the children who've lost a parent. For the mother left without her husband, or the father left without his wife. Lord, wrap your arms around each. Help the children bear their loss and help the single parent carry on in their own sorrow, while helping their children in their need.

Lord, losing a mother or father, a husband or wife, a son or daughter, sucks the very breath and life out of those who are left. Almighty God, shower your love and compassion on those who are drowning in grief. Help each one look to you for strength and help in their circumstances that are beyond comprehension. Lord, after the shock, fear, and anger, loneliness can set in. The survivors are left swimming in a sea of uncertainty.

I ask your help for these, and others being swallowed in grief. Lord, I ask you'd help me know the right words to say or actions to help them. I so often do not know.

Amen

Day 13

Dear Lord God,

Patience is often lacking in this world. Just today someone became impatient with me over something they need not have involved themself in. This wasn't her job or her business. She was not asked to help or be involved in any way, yet she did. She became impatient. I felt attacked.

I know I become impatient with others, too Lord. Sometimes people grate on our nerves when we think they aren't quick enough, paying attention, avoiding their work or task, not listening, and not following through. We get exasperated with each other. Sometimes our impatience comes out as meanness. Forgive us, Lord, when we don't appreciate or we misunderstand another and lose our patience.

I know in my life, Father God, how often you have been patient with me. You've had to nudge me multiple times and wait for a response. You've had to wait while I've learned. You've had to discipline me at times, yet you are never cruel, Lord. You wait on us, teach us, and understand when we are slow to learn. You equip us.

Thank you, Lord God, for every time you've been patient with me. Help me follow your example.

Amen

Day 14

Dear God,

Here I am again. I know you're here with me and will listen and help. My thoughts are scrambled today. I'm not staying on task. I'm allowing outside distractions to deter me from the work I'm trying to accomplish. Maybe I'm trying to do too many things for one day. My focus is wobbly today, Lord.

I try to begin one task, then another chore calls me. I tell myself, "One thing at a time!" I never want to put people off, but I need to quiet my phone from all calls, texts, and emails. It's sometimes that simple…yet so hard. I don't want to feel guilty about it, but sometimes I do.

I know you value every one of us, Lord. I know we need to value each other. So, I try hard, Lord, not to ignore others or discount their needs. It hurts to be ignored. I don't want to be guilty of that. Still, Lord God, there are times I need to sequester myself away and focus on my work. Sometimes I dream of going on a silent retreat. It doesn't have to be formal, just a place away for a few days in solitude. Yet, I know doing such could cause hurt feelings.

The point is, Lord, sometimes I need a time of solitude where I can't be reached except in case of an emergency, or at least only at certain times when I'd turn on my phone. As you know, Lord, my dad used to go away for days of solitude. My spirit must be much like his.

There is a delicate balance, Lord, between socializing and hibernating away. Between vocalizing and staying silent. Between being available and not.

Help me balance these, Lord.

Amen

Day 15

Thank you, Father God!

I thank you for speaking into my spirit and helping me with a relationship situation. Your words of wisdom calmed me, guided me, and taught me a lesson.

I now understand that I don't need to understand this person. I don't need to challenge the lies. I don't need to set this person straight. I only need to love and be kind. I can let the rest go. I can overlook what I might want to challenge. It is not my job to correct or "fix" this person. I understand now that none of these things are my job. They are yours. I can set my boundaries, yet still love, and leave the rest to you.

Lord, thank you for pointing out the fallacy in my thinking. Hearing your words of correction and guidance have lifted a burden. I feel relieved of a load I've been carrying for a long time. I am free and the relationship is healing.

Father, I yearn to hear your voice. I will listen for your words.

Amen

Day 16

Dear God,

I find myself in a bad mood. I was fine and then one remark sent me into a downward spin. It's ridiculous, yet true. I tell myself I shouldn't be so sensitive. I also remind myself to say less. The less said the fewer comments one receives. Just when I feel freedom to express, I get shut down. For me, Lord, that translates… say less, express less, be quiet.

It is good, Lord, to think before we speak, to measure our words carefully. When I don't, I set myself up for a fall—for criticism or simply words that don't set well. Sometimes it's my own fault by sharing unwisely. Sometimes people are careless and cruel in their comments. Either way, I'm now in a subdued, quiet mood. I turned off my phone and other devices. This is partly to concentrate as I work. It's also for self-preservation. I need to distance myself from the many voices—even my own—except for yours, Father God.

You, Lord, are my safe place. You know my foibles and when I err. Yet, you know my thoughts, my heart, and my intent. You understand when others do not. You correct me gently. People can be unkind and harsh in their judgments.

For today, Lord, I shall be quiet and distance myself except from you.

Be near, O Lord God.

Amen

Day 17

Good morning, God.

I have unusual thoughts this morning. I think friends and family might shake their heads if I expressed them. I find myself comparing being human to other life forms you've created.

As I am talking to you, Lord, I'm looking out my second-floor window watching the branches and leaves of a large elm tree sway in the breeze. Patches of blue sky and white clouds can be seen through the limbs and foliage. I wonder—what is it like to be a tree? They are magnificent plants—their huge trunks, life coursing through them and from them. They are life giving. Trees are silent, yet I often feel they have some sort of consciousness. And what of the grasses and flowers, Lord? Each has its own life cycle.

A chickadee just lit on one of the branches, hopping, likely searching for insects in the deeply textured wood. What is it like to be a bird, Lord? It's a life far different from my own. I don't think I'd enjoy being a bird.

There are other small animals that live in our yards and surrounding fields. Each of them has a life unique to its species. What would it be like to be a deer, or skunk, or squirrel, or rabbit, or chipmunk, or fox, or snake? They appear to have live hard lives. Some of them live strange lives.

Lord, you created many types of life, and I am fascinated. I know only what it is to be human. Being human can be a tough life.

Thank you, God, for all your creation.

Help me in the human life you've given me.

I thank you for a life that is connected to you, made in your image.

Amen

Day 18

Hello God.

It is a wonder that you can be everywhere, at every moment, with every person. I thank you for your omnipresence. While I call on you now, in this very moment, you are also with others.

Every day, Lord, is filled with the announcement of illness, impending death, and end-of-life. Every day is filled with words of sorrow and strife. I barely open my eyes or read a word and see expressions of anxiety, depression, fear, and anger. There is a lot to be fearful of in this world, yet Lord you are here and available to each of us. You can lighten our loads as you carry us through our troubles. You can heal us. You can give us peace that passes understanding, and joy in our sorrows. You can hold us up and give us strength to bare our burdens.

If we take your words to heart, O Lord, we can live triumphantly. We can overcome. Even in death, we can overcome because you overcame death for us.

Lord, thank you for dying for me. Thank you for receiving my heart as I gave it to you. Thank you for dwelling within my heart and spirit to guide, to teach, and to soothe.

Thank you, Almighty God, for your presence in my life

Amen

Day 19

I don't understand, Lord.

I started to say hello and good morning to one in my path, but she averted her eyes from me and walked on. I started to begin a conversation, Lord, yet she began talking to another. I opened myself to one I trusted, Lord, you know who. The input and feedback he promised never came. Ever. It's been two years. I am uncomfortable inquiring and haven't.

I have many wonderful friends, Lord. You have sent special people into my life. I am grateful. Yet, there are some who will not connect or engage. It's obvious they do not care for me. I don't know why, but I let it be. Most of the time I would not ask for fear of receiving hurtful comments, or worse being ignored.

I, too, have people I greatly love and others I don't care as much for, but Lord, I try to always keep my word and I do not turn away from one speaking to me.

There are naysayers, Lord. For whatever reasons they do not believe I am fit or qualified to do some of the work I do. That has been a theme in my life when you've called me to something unexpected which to others, and even myself, I did not feel equipped. But, God, you know those stories and you know you called me, and you equipped me and opened doors that only you could. I know when you are in it anything is possible.

You know the reasons, Father, why you've called me to the tasks you have. And while others may not see my potential or my abilities given through you, I will continue. If you put it before me, then I am automatically qualified. It is the same for all of us.

You have called and you have qualified me for the job.

Amen

Day 20

Dear Lord,

The other day my husband and I celebrated our twenty-eighth anniversary. You know our story, Father God. I thank you for a second chance at marriage and for your blessing upon us. There were many, Lord, who did not believe in us or that we would last. Our situation was very messy and greatly misunderstood, O Father God.

Lord, you restored our lives. You gave us a life together that no one predicted. I don't know how you handled all the other players in our scenario, but Lord, you forgave us, restored us, and have blessed us beyond measure. You know me, Lord. You know my heart. You know every longing and every sorrow. You know all the good and bad in me. You know the truth in everything, Lord. That is a great comfort.

Father, you know my worth. You give me my worth. I need look no farther for value but in your eyes and loving all-knowing arms.

Thank you, Father, for the special and close relationship you have given me with my husband. After you, he is my closest friend and knows me better than anyone. Thank you for his love and devotion.

Thank you, Almighty God, for the second chance.

Amen

Day 21

Opinions, Lord, Opinions!

You know how it is, Lord. One says right, the other left. One is for an idea, another opposes it. One votes one way, another the opposite. One likes this, one likes that. We are all so very different.

What I find reasonable, another finds ridiculous and vice versa. What I find exhausting and not worth it, another finds it fun.

Lord, we are indeed very different, we humans. Yet, we are so much alike. We are often seeking the same outcome but our paths to that outcome are quite different. Yet, we cry at the same losses, we hurt over the same circumstances. We find great joy in other circumstances. Our core needs and longings are the same.

Lord, in our great differences may we recognize how much we're alike. May we give room and accept another's way of finding the same answer or reaching the same destination.

But, Father God, there is only one way to you…through Jesus Christ your son. There is the path to you that might be spoken using different words and terminology, but still is the same one path. May all who have not discovered you, and life in you, find the one true God. Once we meet you, God, and have a personal relationship with you, life is changed for the better.

For that I am grateful. Life in you is everything.

Amen

Day 22

Thank you, Lord.

The nicest but most unexpected words find their way to me. A woman in Germany happened to come across and read one of my books. Then another and another. She wrote to me through email, Lord, as you know, and told me how much she related to my stories. What wonderful words for any author to receive.

Also, how amazing that while I was going about my days, this reader in a faraway land was sitting with my book in her hands relating to every word. She was so excited to find another like her that she took the time to write. This was such a blessing receiving her message. Not only that, Lord, we have become friends keeping in touch across the ocean. But not recently.

The past few days she's been on my mind, Father. I have not heard from her, and have not written her recently, until today. Last I heard there was some hardship in her family. Lord, I pray for this, faraway, sister in Christ. Be with her this very minute on this very day and uphold her in any need she may have. Bless her and her family. If possible, Lord, have her receive my message and reply. I would love to know how she's doing.

Thank you, Father God, for the messages I receive unexpectedly, and for the special connections I can make with people through my books. My books can travel farther than I will ever go. Through the gift of books, the words of my stories and testimonies can reach around the world, and other's stories come back to me.

Thank you for every reader. Bless each one, Father.

Amen

Day 23

Thank you, God.

Thank you for our peaceful home and quiet neighborhood. The stillness, existing even during the busy part of the day, is nurturing. As I listen just now, I hear the breeze in the trees and a bird singing. As I continue to listen, I hear a train chugging by. Even the sound of a train is peaceful. I enjoy watching them from the backyard as they move along the hillside.

The quietness of this area fills me with well-being, contentment, and gratitude. I've lived in less peaceful places, Lord, you know. Busy, crowded cities with heavy traffic, fast freeways, gang warfare and gun shots, lives lost; even innocent children caught in crossfire. Millions of people living in one area contributes to strife.

Lord, I thank you for bringing us to a place where life is calm and relaxed. Thank you for allowing our lives to extend into retirement years. When I was young, retirement age seemed forever away, but here I am. It's difficult for the young to imagine becoming old, but it happens to all of us until you call us home.

A squirrel is chattering in the tree, his nest in the upper branches. The leaves are rustling in the breeze. A bird whistles. In the distance I hear a young child's voice as he plays. These are the sounds of a peaceful day, Lord.

Thank you for peacefulness.

Amen

Day 24

Dear God,

I thanked you for peaceful days. Nighttime is even more quiet and peaceful. The stillness under the night sky is breathtaking. In every season the night sky has offered spectacular sights.

It could be considered a nuisance to have to take our dog out at night, but it truly isn't. She is good and smart to call us in her need. I don't mind helping her, Lord. She is beloved. Thank you for her. Her nighttime trips out have allowed me to see spectacular night skies.

One of the most amazing nights was when the sky was so filled with snow clouds that it was as light as day during the deepest part of the night. I had never seen anything like it until living so far north in this snowy state. The snow sky is fascinating, Lord. Thank you for the opportunity to witness these clouds at night. And the blackest of nights, God, when hundreds of stars twinkle and the moon shines brightly, is breath-taking and causes me to feel tiny under such a huge sky. Father, the nights with thunderstorms call to me, even when the dog doesn't need to go out. The lightning, thunder, and wind are spectacular to hear and see, and at times scary. The power of a thunderstorm is to be respected. The nights of calm, or gentle breezes is soothing.

Lord, I've come to love the night sky and the calm of those hours so much that I sometimes feel compelled to go outside in the wee-morning hours for no reason except to experience the quiet reverence I feel under the night sky when all is still. For the most part, both people and animals are still, the motion of the day has stopped. And, while not everyone is resting peacefully, there is a restfulness to the night.

For those suffering sleeplessness, Lord, I asked your peace to fall upon them. For those who would benefit from stepping outside to experience the stillness and calmness of the night, help them take the step to do so. The deepness of the night can be healing, Lord. I've experience it. When all is quiet, we can experience you best and our spirits can be soothed.

Thank you for the healing power of the night, Lord.

Amen

Day 25

Dear Lord,

Thank you for your constant presence. I feel your nearness. I experience you through nature every morning. I experience peace and joy in my heart and soul because of your companionship toward me. I hear your still small voice whisper to me. You speak words of affirmation and guidance. You speak ideas into my spirit to help me accomplish my goals, or a task you have for me.

Lord God, I know you hear me when I speak to you, and I know you hear the unspoken thoughts and longings of my heart. Thank you for your spirit who intervenes on my behalf. I know, God, that you are aware of my every moment and my every thought. You know what I need before I ask.

Thank you, Lord, for answering my prayers…for understanding what I express. Thank you, Almighty God, for your voice, for talking to me. Your words are inaudible, but words, nonetheless. At those moments when I hear you speak, my spirit soars! Who am I, Lord, that you should take the time to notice me, hear me, and even speak to me? This is beyond wonderful, and I thank you, Lord God.

May all know you.

Amen

Day 26

Lord,

There is another shift taking place in my life. Throughout life there are times when age changes things. Children live in one world, teenagers in another. Young adults, single or married, have their reality. Then, Lord, middle age comes. It's different, still, and is one time when many notice a lot of changes in life. Then, Lord, there are the senior years and growing older. I am there.

There is a definite sense that younger adults look at me, speak to me, and act toward me as an older person, as I once did toward older adults when I was younger. They treat me as one they consider might need extra help. I am treated with respect as a youngster might be taught to treat older people. I am seen as an "old" person. This is a strange feeling and observation, Lord. Things have flipped.

Not only that, Lord God, but my elderly father is now needing the same help from me that he once gave to me. I am now the adult, he the child. This is a strange reversal of roles. It is not intentional. It just happens. As he once held my hand to steady my small legs, I now hold his hand to steady his weakening legs. He has entered a new stage as I have entered a new stage.

Lord, I don't feel old, and I don't think I act especially old, but things have changed within me. And societies perception of me is now as being one of the older generations. Long gone are the days of my youth. My babies are grown. They are in or are approaching middle age. That does make me an old person, I guess. I am Gramma.

Lord, when I was a child old age seemed far away. It seemed it would be a long time before I was a grandmother. It was so far away I could not fathom it at all, yet here I am. Many years have passed, Lord, and I am truly on the far end of life. I could live thirty to forty more years. Only you know when my last day will come.

I've had a good life, Lord. I'm enjoying life still. It has not been without trials and struggles, but overall, I've had a wonderful life. I'm eager to live more of it, if it is in your plan, Almighty God.

Thank you for the years past. Thank you for this very day. Thank you for all future days you may allow.

Amen

Day 27

Here I am again, Lord.

I'm so glad I can come to you any time for any reason. Some days, I'm tired and unproductive. Other days, I'm full of energy and filled with creativity. Sometimes every interruption is an annoyance. Other days, I welcome interruptions. Today is steady and productive. Thank you for this day.

People tell me I am very busy, but I'm not too busy. You know, Lord God, that I do not like being overly busy and fight against it. Some weeks, like this week, there are extra activities on my calendar. They're not recurring. Other times my calendar is free of extracurricular activities for weeks on end, especially in the winter. Summer is the busiest season, and it is summertime now.

Tomorrow will be a busy day and I am preparing ahead. Lord, I ask a special blessing on those of us who will be taking the stage tomorrow night at the outdoor park, to introduce ourselves as part of the local writer's group and read some of our work. We want our town to know about our group and our books. It's a privilege to share.

I pray for good weather, a receptive crowd, and for each of us who will speak.

Thank you for the opportunity.

Amen

Day 28

Dear Lord,

There are so many needs. Day after day I hear of someone who's become very sick. I hear of one mangled in a terrible accident, one who's committed suicide, or tried. I hear of disease aggressively attacking someone's body and threatening life. I hear of so much pain, and depression, and of those who cannot sleep. They struggle through their days with fatigue and fuzzy minds. I hear of people not only driving drunk but driving sleepy. Accidents occur.

Lord, we are a nation of busyness yet sleeplessness. We are a nation of strife not peace. We are a people who brand ourselves with whatever pain, sorrow, disease, or trouble that afflicts us. As a wise friend mentioned, we allow our afflictions to become our identity.

Father God, help us to see ourselves as more than a disease, an invalid, a griever, a struggler. Lord God, help us to see ourselves as you do, with the identity you gave us upon our creation. We are not our trials, our sins, our illnesses, or any other label that we accept. We are who you have created us to be.

Lord, cause us to know who we truly are in your eyes.

Amen

Day 29

Lord,

In some ways this has been a great day. I've been productive at a steady pace. I've accomplished things at home, things away from home, and at my desk.

Lord, this has not been a good day for exercise or in my meals. I am all off balance today in those areas, yet God, those areas are important for my health. It is my desire to exercise every day and eat well and light. I didn't accomplish either of those today. It's rare I miss a day of exercise, but I did today. I could have made better food choices, but I didn't.

I know, Lord, that these are my decisions. I also know that messing up for one or two days is not worth beating myself up. I won't do that. I'll do better tomorrow. There's always a new day with a new start.

Thank you, Lord, for new days, new starts, a chance to try again in the smallest and most important of situations. Thank you for your constant compassion, help, guidance, forgiveness, and understanding.

I praise you Lord God Almighty.

Amen

Day 30

Hello Lord,

I am feeling grateful and fulfilled. I am grateful to you. You have called me to work that I love. You have filled me with passion for my work. I enjoy the effort. Though I can get tired, the work is not tiring. Sometimes I want to work long after it's time to quit for the day. Sometimes I want to work in the middle of the night. I am often most creative in the dark of night.

You gave me this passion in my musical journey, and you have given me the same passion in my writing journey. Lord, it makes all the difference in the world to follow your callings, rather than to try to live and operate outside of them. This is a truth I have learned. This is the truth I hope and pray all people will know. It is for us and for you that we follow your callings. It is for the benefit of all mankind.

Lord, thank you for helping me and equipping me. So much of what you've called me to do I stepped into unprepared. I wondered why you were asking me to do the jobs in the first place. I was not prepared, but you brought help and training for me, to do all you asked. Thank you for the fun and wonderful relationships I've made along the way. I have been blessed by many, Lord. You have uplifted me in so many ways. In the times I feel deserted by people, I know you have not deserted me, Lord God. You have never left me alone.

Thank you, Father.

Amen

Day 31

Lord God,

This storm is powerful. Thunder rumbles and booms, and lightning cracks the sky. Rain and hail fall heavily and loudly. The wind is fierce, bending the limbs of large, substantial trees. We humans and animals alike have tucked ourselves safely into our respective homes. We hide away from the mighty power of the weather.

The storm is magnificent, Lord, but brings a hint of fear. The force of the storm is far greater than we are. I am in awe of what you have created. I am aware of how small and weak I am against such a storm. I am at its mercy—at your mercy, Lord.

The storm is exciting, too, God. The sounds, the earthy smells, the strength of the wind as it surges. The darkened sky even in daylight hours. It is ominous. It is humbling. I bow to the storm and its might. I bow to you, Almighty God, you who has set the storms in motion, and set the sunshine, and moonlight, and stars.

Lord God, you are the Creator…of all heaven and earth.

I bow to you.

Amen

Day 32

Dear God,

Thank you! You heard my thoughts and longings and blessed me, even though I didn't directly speak to you about my wish. Just a day after I was sadly contemplating why no Johnny Jump Ups had sprouted in my flower beds or yard, this morning I saw one! I was so elated when I caught sight of the tiny beauty.

It seemed odd, Lord, that after years of watching these small flowers pop up here, there, and everywhere, I would not see even one. You knew my disappointment, Lord. You heard the lamenting in my spirit. You understood the joy that seeing those tiny blossoms brings me.

Lord, it didn't matter that I did not ask you to bring the Johnny Jump Ups to my yard. You gave them to me because of the desire in my heart. It is these gifts, loving God, that remind me how much you care for me—even in the smallest of ways. As you have done before, you gifted me with an expression of your love for no reason except to simply bestow love upon me.

Thank you, Lord, for knowing me and loving me.

Amen

Day 33

Lord God,

Help me. Today is difficult. I'm in a bad mood. I'm down on myself. My self-esteem is weak. My self-image is twisted. And today, Lord, I feel picked on.

Lord God, I am not being heard. No one is listening. Before I finish a thought, I'm being talked over. So much talk and so little listening. This is the way of the world. The chatter is overwhelming. I wish every voice would go silent for a moment and listen.

Lord, if the world would become still maybe we could hear your voice loud and clear. So much thought and wisdom get lost in the noise of the world. It becomes deafening. It becomes disheartening when listeners are few.

Father God, thank you for listening.

Amen.

Day 34

Oh Lord,

A dear friend died today. He was dear to so many of us. You know who he is. He was your servant. He was a loving and encouraging man. His care for each of us shined through, Lord. Bless him in eternity.

I can only imagine, Almighty God, what it was like when my friend stood before you and saw your face. I know my friend, Lord. I know he bowed before you. I know you raised him up and welcomed him into his eternal home with you.

Father, bless my friend. Thank you for the friend he was to so many. He was your good and faithful servant. Thank you for the gift of eternal life in your kingdom.

Amen

Day 35

Holy Father,

You are the Lord God Almighty. You are the creator of all. You are omniscient and omnipresent. You, Lord God, are Holy. You are to be praised and revered.

Lord, we pray constantly for all our needs and wants. We pray constantly for our health and for healing. We ask for deliverance from depression, anxiety, and fear. We pray for jobs and income. We pray for material needs. We pray for safety. We constantly ask your help, Lord. We constantly ask for guidance. We ask, ask, ask, Lord God, and even beg. We have many needs and desires, and you are loving, kind, and compassionate toward us.

Almighty God, we forget that you are holy, and powerful, and worthy to be praised. We are told in your words of scripture that we are to bow to you and praise you. We are to follow your commands. We are to listen to your voice and follow.

Forgive us, Lord. Forgive me, Lord, when I forget to express my words of gratitude and thanksgiving to you. Forgive me, Lord, when I fail to listen. Listening to you and following your plan is for my benefit. You always know best, Lord God. You are all-knowing.

Forgive me Lord when I fail you.

Amen

Day 36

Lord God,

Thank you for every provision. Thank you for the new work you have given me. I have long known I'm not a nine-to-five type person. It was wonderful being self-employed thirty years, and now being retired—after seven years of nine-to-five-punch-a-time-clock-work—I am elated to be working on my own time schedule again, doing work I love. Thank you for the opportunity, Lord.

Thank you, Lord, for the ability to do the work. You have equipped me with people and programs to learn from, helped me obtain equipment I need to do my work, and have given me the health and energy to do it. I praise you for all this.

Lord, I feel joy in my work. I know this comes from you. Thank you for the open doors, for showing me yet another plan for me and for every encouragement along the way.

My days are filled with lovely things.

Thank you, Father.

Amen

Day 37

Father God,

I'm excited! I am getting a new toy. Even adults like toys, Lord, as you know.

I've been afraid to ride my bicycle for fear of falling and breaking a bone. My bones are less strong these days, Lord. You know that, too. But, oh, how I've enjoyed bike riding throughout my life—the wind in my face and hair, cycling and gliding along. I've missed that the past few years, not riding as much. Now I'm ready to ride but need something safer than my two-wheeler.

My three-wheel bike will arrive this week. I am eager to try it out. I'll have no fear of falling and getting hurt. With the big basket between the back wheels, Lord, I could carry groceries or other items.

Thank you, Father, for helping me afford this new toy. Thank you for caring about our every wish and need. I am grateful.

Amen

Day 38

Father,

Today begins a new month. This year is passing quickly. It's difficult to believe Christmas is less than five months away. It doesn't seem possible. It's a little unsettling, Lord, to see how fast time is passing. The months fly by one after the other.

Already, Lord, the grasses, plants, and the air itself are hinting of fall. I look forward to fall and winter, but it seems summer has just begun. Not to be pessimistic, Father, but before long we here will all be gone from this world…memories of others. It's an odd and sometimes frightening thought.

Every day, Lord, I know I'm one day closer to meeting you. I don't expect to see you anytime soon, but only you, Almighty God, know when my time on this earth will be up. It is an ominous thought, yet a joyful thought to know I will be with you.

Help me, Lord, to live my life to the fullest, in the ways you would have me live out my days. Help me be a blessing to at least someone. Prepare me for my future with you, Lord, while I continue my days here. The world is a mess, Father, yet I do love life and find much beauty here in your creations.

Thank you for life now and eternal.

Amen

Day 39

Dear Father,

My heart goes out to the old among us. There are many who are living to be exceptionally old. My own father, Lord, is one of those. So many friends and family have passed on before these of such advanced years and they are left with distant memories.

Though many older folks have trouble with memory loss, Lord, they can remember far back into their younger years. That is a blessing, because so many have fond memories of those long-ago days, even if they were difficult times. While their memory fades, Father, thank you for blessing so many with pleasant memories from their youth. These memories seem to bring them joy, even if with some pain.

Bless the elderly, Father. Help them in their old-age difficulties. Give us patience and fill us with love and kindness for these who are living out their last years and are often lonely. Remind us, Father, that we too are growing older. We will be in their shoes one day if we should live so long.

Give extra of your love, Father, to those you have blessed with a long life.

They have great value and purpose.

Amen

Day 40

Lord,

I fear for young children growing up in today's world. I know evil has always been present in the world and times have not been easy throughout the generations, but it seems the world is a scarier place today. There is much to deal with that we have never dealt with before. There is so much children see and hear that their young minds are not ready to understand.

Father, be with the parents of today. Help them as they raise their children. Give them wisdom, Lord. As you draw them unto you, I pray they will seek you. Parenting is a difficult job. Without you it must be a treacherous path.

Father God, be with teachers and guide them as they teach their classrooms of students. Within the limits they are bound, help them teach well and wisely. Fill them with love for children and youth.

Father, help every child grow to know you. You created them for this time, Lord. Watch over and care for them in this world of scrambled beliefs. Help each child and youth come to know your truth, Father God.

Amen

Day 41

Lord God,

Thank you for animals. Thank you for pets. They bring so much joy. I fall deeply in love with my pets, Lord. You know that. You know how we grieve when a pet dies. Oh Lord, it hurts so much to say good-bye to our animal companions. They live on in our hearts.

Our beloved dog, Melody, is gone now, Lord. You know what a wonderful soul she was. I've had many dogs, but she was exceptional. She was a wonderful gift. Thank you for bringing her into our lives, so unexpectedly. We loved her deeply and we miss her.

Thank you for our cat, Merri. Our one and only pet now. She is a special treasure to us. I've had many cats, Lord, you know. This cat is one of the best. I love how she reaches for me, how she snuggles with me, and how she seeks our affection and gives affection.

Pets soothe us. They calm us. They accept us. They depend on us. It's wonderful to have someone to care for, to meet their needs, even if a pet. We all need to be needed and we all need to be loved. Animals do that for us so well by the way you created them.

Thank you, God, for animals and pets.

Amen

Day 42

Almighty God,

What a magnificent morning! I didn't want to get up so early, but I'm so glad I did. There's something about seeing the sunrise, feeling the cool morning breeze, and the way the trees, grasses, plants, and animals act and look in the early hours that is enriching. It feeds my soul, Lord.

This morning was exceptional! I would have missed it if I'd lounged. The breeze quickly became a full wind, and the rustling in the trees became the music of nature. It was interesting how different the sound was in the different trees. The cottonwood trees and elm trees played a different tune. The former, loud and crisp, the latter, muted and murmurous. Remarkable!

The sun came up, but every sunrise is unique, and todays was its own unique rise. It was a little later—as everyday it arrives just a minute later than the day before. The days are slowly becoming shorter.

I can feel and see hints of fall, Lord. The grasses are fading from deep and lush to pale green. It has almost stopped growing. The air faintly contains the feel and scent of fall. I saw yellow leaves in several trees this morning.

Lord God, the magic of the changing seasons is beginning. It's subtle but it is unmistakable.

I closed my eyes as I sat on my swing. The morning sounds of birds were few, but the wind blew strong and reminded me of another place. The ebb and flow of the wind in the trees sounded remarkably like the ebb and flow of waves on an ocean beach. The wind felt coastal.

This morning was invigorating and inspiring, Lord. I'm so glad I got up. Thank you for urging me to rise.

Thank you for the astounding morning experiences, God.

Amen

Day 43

Lord God,

Some days are so frustrating. So many obstacles. It can be trying, Lord. It's difficult when people keep changing their minds, or don't follow through with what they've promised. There are plenty of times we can't help changes—they're out of our hands. But people can vacillate for no good reason or fail to follow through.

Lord, I know for every frustration I've felt, I have also frustrated another. Forgive me when I fail someone else. Help me to be true to my word or not promise at all. Help me to say no when I mean no and when I say yes to follow through cheerfully. Help us all to be people of our word.

Lord, above all fill us with patience for each other. Help us to forgive one another and not hold grudges. Help us to keep our promises, as broken promises hurt. I thank you, God, for your loving patience, kindness, and the forgiveness you've shown me. Thank you for every promise you have made, kept, and will keep.

May I grow in following your example.

Amen

Day 44

Lord,

Today is thirty-two years since my mother died. We have no idea why you took her so soon, so young, or why she had to suffer so greatly. I have now outlived my mom by five years. I often wonder what the past thirty-two years would have been like if Mom were here. The years would have been different, for sure. What has she been doing all these years, Lord? I had a dream that you gave her the job of making rocks for use here on earth in our gardens. She was creative maybe you've given her creative work.

Lord, it's now been over two years since my brother passed. He was far too young to die, too. Why did my brother have to suffer twenty-five years with one disease and then be afflicted with another? He suffered a long time, Lord. You allowed him to suffer those life-threatening illnesses that took so much freedom from him. Yet, I know you were with him during all his struggles.

There were many things both my mother and brother enjoyed, Almighty God, yet they were stripped away. I'm sad they suffered, but know they found peace. I know you love them.

I thank you, God, for the health I enjoy. I know it could end. I'm grateful for each day.

Amen

Day 45

Lord,

I feel fear already creeping up in me and there are still ten days before I am faced with the challenge. Lord, you know I am afraid of road travel. You know I am afraid in cars. You know my fears of all that could happen to cause a terrible accident. Lord, why must I travel? I don't want to, yet I must. At least I think I must. I've made a promise. I don't want to make such a promise ever again. Don't I have the choice, Lord?

In ten days, we must travel across the state 224 miles. Father, that is so far and so long to be on the road. I'm afraid. I know to most this seems an irrational fear, but I have lived with it my entire life. You know my fear. Please take it away, Lord God.

I remember, God, how you came to me in my fear before and allowed me to see your angels around our car protecting us with their mighty wings, and watchful faces looking forward down the road. The angel on my side even looked back and smiled at me, Lord. Thank you for that vision. Almighty God, please send your angels again on our days of travel to and from our destination. Let them keep us safe. Lord, I give you my fear.

Thank you for your gracious care.

Amen

Day 46

Dear God,

Thank you for my recent accomplishments. I know you are the giver of such things. Thank you for your guidance, open doors, and leading the right people into my path. Thank you for the behind-the-scenes opportunities you were working out unbeknownst to me.

I've learned, Lord, that when I step back and allow you to be alive in me wonderful things happen that bring great joy. Thank you for knowing me and working out the details of my life. Your plans are always the best. Thank you for taking my steps and guiding them into your path and plans. If I begin to stray, please pull me back to your way.

The longer I know you, Lord God, the more I want to know you. The more I want to know the plans you have laid out for me, the more I want to follow them. You have never let me down, Lord. It is easier and easier to trust you because of the faithfulness you have consistently shown.

Thank you, Lord, for every good gift.

Amen

Day 47

Dear God,

Why are some people so rude? Why must some people completely ignore one person while gushing over another? Lord, you know, I have been in this position many times—completely ignored, even when standing right alongside the other, involved in the same work or activity. It makes one feel invisible. It's not a nice feeling at all!

And Lord, as I've asked before, why will a person be so rude as to totally ignore what one has said or asked, or promised something then brush it off as if the person's words, request, and their own promise in response meant nothing. It is rude and hurtful, Father. Maybe even hateful.

Is it forgetfulness, or selfishness, or meanness? How can a person totally turn away from a greeting, or act as if they're listening and engaging, then walk away oblivious to what was said or asked?

Lord, any answer is better than no answer. Ignoring someone is a grievous act. It's the worst. No wonder we are taught as children to ignore those bullying or belittling us, so that we don't fuel their fire. Ignoring can squelch such behavior, but it also squelche a person's spirit. It is the height of unkindness. Father God, help me to never ignore another.

Thank you for never ignoring me.

Amen

Day 48

God,

It has been a beautiful day! Dawn and sunrise were exceptionally nice. The early hours are so peaceful, Lord, and your presence is powerful. The majesty of all you've created seems accentuated in the early morning hours.

The quietness of the morning is soothing and prepares us for the busyness and noise of the day. To connect with you early is a mighty experience and sets the tone for the entire day. It helps us through the rough spots.

Lord God, I feel there is much you want to say to me that I have not yet heard. Help me be open, and ready, eager, and willing to hear you, God. I long to hear your voice. Help my spirit and heart be open to hear you.

Thank you for the beauty of this morning. Thank you for being in it.

Thank you for your quiet patience and understanding as we learn and grow—sometimes oh so slowly.

Thank you, Lord, for this magnificent day.

Amen

Day 49

Almighty God,

When the days are long, full of sorrow, and the future looks black, fill us with your peace and hope for better days. Grief is heavy, Lord. It is a great burden to bear unless you lift us up into your care. Prompt us, Lord God, to seek you in our darkest hours when our pain is so great we can't figure out how we'll carry on.

You alone, Lord, know our heartache and the darkness in our aching spirits. You alone, Father, know the deepest recesses of our pain. You, God, are our help and refuge like no human can be.

Lord, you know every scar we bear. You know every trigger that will drop us to our knees all over again in wretched pain and sorrow. You see, and feel, every tear that runs down our sadden faces. You know every conflict within us.

Lord, you alone can heal us. Though it may take time, you can and will walk us through every treacherous step of each day until our pain is bearable and only faint scars are left. These scars will not only cause us to remember the feelings of darkness and abandonment but will remind us of your care and healing as we had trod helplessly through the barren soil of grief. Our scars will show emotional and spiritual healing and one day will become faint.

We will know your hope, your peace, and the fullness of joy.

Amen

Day 50

Dear Lord,

My heart is light. There was a time when it was so saturated with sorrow and grief that I could barely breathe. Tears fell ceaselessly. I was on guard every moment of every day expecting more pain around every corner. Sleep was fitful.

But, Lord, you healed my heart! I thank you and praise you for carefully and lovingly holding my heart in your hands while I healed. I no longer fear. I know that even if betrayal and deep hurt come my way again, I will survive and carry on. In a sense, I would not care. Not because I will not hurt, but because I know you will be there holding me up every step of the way. I fear not, therefore my pain will be less.

I learned, Lord, that peace and joy come from only you. People will hurt us, intentionally or not. We cannot fully rely on our friends and family. They are not perfect, as you are Holy God.

You, Lord, are our security in this world.

I shall not fear.

Amen

Day 51

Lord God,

I am filled with a grateful heart. I am in awe of you. Thank you for being available to me on any day at every moment. Thank you for listening to me no matter my mood, frame of mind, or attitude.

I am thankful to be able to talk to you when I am fearful and nervous, or fearless and calm. When I feel supported or let down, when I am tired or energetic, when I am confused or have clear thinking, when I am crying or laughing, angry or peaceful, content or discontent, eager or sluggish, in sickness or health.

Lord, no matter the situation you are there. I can call on you and you come to me. You are my closest friend. You have the answers to all. You are my guide, my teacher, my conscience, my rebuker, my support, my help, my counselor, my Holy God, and Savior.

I am filled with gratefulness.

Amen

Day 52

Father,

We are sick: Viruses, bacteria, cancer, heart attacks, strokes, blood clots, rashes, mental illness, dementia, Alzheimer's, crippling, atrophied muscles, joint ailments, hearing loss, loss of sight, diseases of all kinds—too many to name. We are sick, Father. Help us in our physical frailties. There is little we can do about them ourselves. Doctors try and doctors can bring cures to a degree, but not like you, Lord.

I know illness and disease is part of our fallen world. We must live with it and care for ourselves as best as we can. But, Father God, we need you. We need your intervention and healing.

Lord, when you don't heal and it's our time to leave this world, be by our sides. Hold us as we struggle with our last breaths. Help us as we say good-bye, or others say good-bye to us.

Take your children to your heavenly home, Father. Be by the side of those who mourn.

It is the way of earthly life. Help us understand and help us bear it.

We look to you.

Amen

Day 53

Oh Lord God,

It's a tough day. Frustration has overwhelmed me. Anger is brewing. How can a day begin so nicely and deteriorate so quickly? I am tired and motivation is waning.

I feel defeated, Lord. There is suddenly too much to do. Endless voices speak their opinions. There are new ways of doing things. I don't necessarily want new ways. Learning is endless to be able to accomplish my goals. Today, I am tired of learning. I observe some of the new ways and I don't like them. They tire me and often annoy me.

Lord God, again I feel the chatter never stops. It's deafening. I desire peace and quiet. I need solitude. I have hidden myself away right now to find silence and to seek you. You have promised when we seek you, you will come. When we pray earnestly from our hearts you come. Lord, you have promised you will hear us.

Father, hear me today as I seek you in my quiet place. Almighty God, speak to me. I want to hear your voice. Forgive my negative emotions toward others and calm my spirit as I seek your path and truth for me.

Thank you, Father.

Amen

Day 54

Father God,

I was awake only ten minutes when my phone and computer were bombarding me with messages of sadness, death, emergencies, and strife. Lord, only minutes into my day and the world was groaning and moaning. I began to grumble over all I was hearing. Save us, Father.

I know, Lord, that people are suffering in every imaginable way. Some of those sufferings I have never known, but I have experienced my own difficult and even tortuous days. You know I have, Lord.

Some people plaster their troubles all over social media or will announce them to any who will listen. Some, Father, are more private and keep their business to themselves. Not everyone shares their every struggle, triumph, or emotions.

Lord, this I know. When I unable or unwilling to share my hurts or trials with even those closest to me, I know I can come to you. You are my safe place. You are the one who fully understands me—my fears, heartache, pain, struggles, and weariness. You also understand my joy, my happiness, my creativity, my peacefulness.

Almighty God, you are my confidant and giver of all that is good. You truly do turn ashes to beauty. You truly do heal our emotional pain, and more. Lord God, you bring peace in chaos, joy in sorrow, and lift us with your mighty hand of strength. You ease our sadness and strife.

I praise and thank you, Almighty God, for this.

Amen

Day 55

Dear God,

I'm tired today. Everything is more difficult when I'm tired. I feel badly for the many who do not sleep at night, who toss and turn fitfully even when sleep does come. I slept last night. I don't suffer sleep deprivation, but I am sometimes worn out physically or emotionally. My brain is on overload.

Lord, Jesus suffered weariness, too. I know he suffered in all the ways I do. In the Bible there are stories of his sadness, exhaustion, the need for solitude, praying to you Father for his needs. I know he suffered great hardship, hunger, and physical pain. Father God, remind me of Jesus's human struggles whenever I begin to complain or feel sorry for myself. Remind me, Lord, that Jesus suffered all.

Remind me, Lord, that Jesus suffered the ultimate pain and price to save us. None of us will ever hang on a cross and die carrying the weight of all the sin of the world. None of us will overcome death and rise again.

Lord God, I am tired today. I know it is nothing compared to what Jesus suffered or what even other humans have suffered, but it is my fatigue and I know you care.

Help me this day, Heavenly Father.

Amen

Day 56

Lord God,

Thank you for this day to recover from the extra busyness of the past few weeks. The sunrise was warm and welcoming as I enjoyed the early morning in my backyard haven. The stillness of the hour was rejuvenating.

The morning was perfect for healing. It was quiet, the sky blue, the breeze cool, but the early sunshine warm. The birds and other animals were busy tending to their needs. The grasshoppers and crickets chirped their late summer songs. Trains rumbled by—the sight and sound of them soothing.

I'm grateful, Lord, that I can enjoy slow mornings and soak up the pleasures of the early hours. I'm grateful for the years you've given me. I treasure them and look forward to more if you should allow it. It can be difficult here in our earthly world, but it isn't all bad. You've given us much to enjoy and you sustain us through every day.

I thank you, God.

Amen

Day 57

Father,

I wonder how you see children as compared to adults. Little children are so innocent, Lord. They live in their own world, so unaware of what awaits them as teens and adults. They are precious. Protect the children, Father. They need you now and for all that will come.

Children grow into teenagers and what a difference there is. Teenagers have difficult years to maneuver through. Lord, help them. They are no longer innocent, yet not mature, either. They are often confused. Help the teenagers, Father, as they grow into adulthood. Help them stay on track for goodness rather than corruption. They need you.

Adults need you, too, Lord. We may need you the most. We are charged with raising our children. It's not an easy road. Adults have their own struggles, in addition to dealing with the struggles of their children. Adults have experience, but not always the right answers. Adults may not always act wisely or know what to do.

God, as we grow older new difficulties arise. As seniors we may need help and become burdens to our adult children who are still in the midst of their own parenting responsibilities and may become overwhelmed. Lord, every age has its drama and difficulties, yet every age can approach you for comfort, help, guidance, and wisdom,

Father God, be with the children, the teens, the adults, and the seniors.

Everyone at every age needs you.

Amen

Day 58

Hello again Father,

I am rethinking my goals and what is most important. I ask your help as I do this. What others think I should do, what I think I should do, and what you think I should do can be very different. I need to know what you think, Lord; what you choose for my path. The best answer is not always clear, especially when others are persuasive.

I know myself well enough to know what is too much. I'm not afraid to try new ideas and scrap the ones that don't work out well. Lord, I need to focus my energy in the best places. I want quality in my work more than quantity.

In all areas of life, I need your guidance. In all work and careers, people need your guidance. May we all seek you, Lord God, to know where we should place the bulk of our energy.

I asked today, Father, that you guide me as I seek to do my best within your will.

Thank you.

Amen

Day 59

Lord,

Sometimes the smallest things excite me. I heard cicadas today! I've never heard them here in town, but I did today, right outside the window in the big elm tree. All of nature is awe inspiring. Thank you for the gift of the cicadas.

I bought more yarn today, and another book. They will bring much pleasure in my off hours when I relax.

I placed four more solar lights in the yard today. They shine so nicely at night, lighting the path to our door and accentuating small corners of the yard. They sparkle.

There is one, single Johnny Jump Up in my flower garden this year, Lord. That little flower is precious. Thank you for the one.

Our little granddaughter gave such warm, tight hugs the other day. I love her little arms around me and her great big smile when she and her grandpa hug. Thank you for her, your precious creation.

When I rode my new bike, the wind blew in my face and through my hair. Riding brings such a feeling of freedom.

Thank you, Lord, for these simple gifts and pleasures. They are the highlights of my day.

Amen

Day 60

Dear Lord, God Almighty,

The sun has set. The night air is cooling as the sun sinks further below the horizon. Darkness will envelope us soon. Stillness will descend upon us. We will soon quiet ourselves and prepare for sleep.

Bless each person as we lie down for the night. I ask for peaceful sleep and pleasant dreams for all. I ask that angels watch over us as we sleep.

Lord, I pray for all who will experience restlessness or tragedy on this very night. Cover them with your great compassion. Help those who don't know you to seek you. If they seek you, I know they will find you. Lord don't turn away from those in need on this night.

Another day has passed. Sustain us through the night and prepare our hearts and minds for a new day.

Goodnight Father.

Amen

Day 61

Lord,

Where is our dog? Is she with you? I miss our beloved Melody who left us not so long ago. Lord, she was your creation, and a marvelous one. Dogs have souls. Where is she, God? Is she with you? Will we see her again? I so hope to see her again. I pray she is running free and happy—no illness or physical disabilities.

Where do our beloved pets go, Father? Why can't we know? Where is Calico, Buffy, Smokey, Mr. Jones, Fergie, Tudor, Happy, and Melody? There were others through the years, too. All these pets were dearly loved. It hurt to lose them.

Now we only have our kitty, Merri. Thank you for her health and affection. I know she loves us, as we love her. I know she misses Melody. Pets grieve, as we do.

Where is our Melody, Lord? Will we see her again?

Thank you for the years we had her. You know she helped me through grief.

She was a precious soul, a special, unexpected gift.

Thank you for knowing we needed her and how much we would love her and she us.

Where is Melody, Lord? I hope she is in your eternal kingdom.

Amen

Day 62

Father God,

It has been a productive two days. My work kept me busy, but I met my deadline! I'm happy and excited that I was able to complete the job on the final day and meet my goal. It took almost every minute of the last day, but it is finished on time. I want to run around calling out, "I did it. I did it!" It feels good to accomplish what I set out to do.

My brain is tired, Lord. I worked hard mentally. Some jobs take a lot of mental energy. Writing and website work certainly do. Now I need to take a walk and get physical exercise and rest my mind. Thank you for my health, that I can work both my brain and body.

Thank you, Father, for helping me complete my task and meet my goal. I know that all things are possible through you, and I know you helped me. A daunting task can feel overwhelming and even impossible, but it is completed.

Thank you, Father for sustaining me.

Amen

Day 63

Lord,

Thank you for the days of goals met and celebration. After long, hard work it's nice to recognize achievement. I know, God, that you are in my work with me. It is because of you I can complete the work and reach my goals. You continue to amaze me with what you allow in my life and work.

Thank you, Father, for the days when encouragement comes. Thank you for the positive words that come my way from time to time. They are salve to a weary soul. They lift me up and fuel my fire to continue.

Lord God, thank you for the "mountain top" days, because darker days in the valley will surely return. The darker days help me appreciate the bright days and the bright days bring wonder and joy enough to carry me through the next valley.

Thank you, Lord, for never letting me linger too long in the valleys. During each dark day I trust you for lighter days…and they come.

Today I thank you for a day of light and celebration.

Amen

Day 64

Holy God,

Never let me forget that you are holy. You are the creator of all, holy, just, and mighty. Lord, you are to be praised and glorified. You are to be acknowledged. In so doing, I benefit.

Lord, we so often speak of your love, compassion, care, provision, and answered prayer, but you are much more than our benevolent Father. You are Almighty God, omnificent, omnipresent, and in control of all. You are a jealous God and want each of us to bow down to only you. Only you are deserving of such. You are the one true God.

Father God, I owe everything to you. May I bow in your presence.

Find me worthy, Lord God, for I am yours.

Amen

Day 65

Lord,

Sometimes I do not want to do what I must do. I am overwhelmed by the tasks of this week— one of which I should have declined but allowed myself to be urged into saying "Yes." Father, I do not want to follow through with my word, but I must. It would be terribly wrong to back out. Please give me grace in this promise. Give me the energy and ability to do it well.

There is so much in this world tugging at us. So much. Sometimes I get in over my head, though I make every effort to avoid being overloaded. Lord God, help me know when to say "yes" and when to say "no". Help me to not answer hastily, but to think each situation through. Help me know my limits—not everything is as easy as it was in my younger years.

Lord, I find myself longing for this week to be over—to be past the hurdles staring me in the face. Grant me peace and joy amidst the challenges.

Thank you for your help.

Amen

Day 66

Father God,

I'm excited to see the seasons changing. Summer is fading as fall is clearly moving in. Every season is a gift, Lord. I appreciate the changes in weather, temperature, and scenery in this part of the country. Spring with new life and warming sunshine, summer in its lush green, fall with its many colors and cooler air. Then God, the winter landscape of white is breathtaking. Winter will soon be here. I will welcome it.

There is a restfulness, Lord, in fall and winter. All plant and animal life cease growth and activity. All becomes quieter, and more peaceful. I appreciate the break from yard care and summer busyness to the more restful seasons of nature, Thank you, Lord God, for these variations throughout the year.

With the seasonal changes, the holidays will come. Remind us to rest even within the excitement and hubbub they bring. Lord, help us slow our pace and not miss the peacefulness of fall and winter. Help us keep our focus on the importance of these holidays and not allow ourselves to be overcome with stress from too many activities.

Father God, as all of nature winds down to rest during the long, cold, winter, allow our spirits to rest, too.

Amen

Day 67

Dear Lord,

Today is the day I must meet the obligation I agreed to months ago. I wish I'd thought it through a while longer. I might have said "no". But, Lord, I said, "yes'. Please help me today to meet this obligation with a smile and good attitude. Not only that, Father, help me be able to physically carry it out well. It is a challenge to play piano with arthritic hands.

Lord, you know my challenges. You know what I struggle with now that I didn't struggle with when I was younger. We can find new states of grace as we age, Father. We can be far more capable than we realize, especially when you are in it with us. There is also the fact of accepting the changes that take place as we age allowing us to work within new limitations.

Lord, help me realize what I can and should continue and where I need to change the expectations of myself. There are some uncertainties and I need clarity.

I ask your help, Father.

Amen

Day 68

Lord God Almighty,

Another death has occurred. It's often shocking news. We often don't stop to realize that people are dying daily, just as new babies are being born every day. Daily deaths occur around us and around the world. Lord, we don't often stop to remember that our own deaths will come. It is a sobering thought, yet the absolute truth.

God Almighty, I know we should not be surprised when people die. It is a sad part of life, but it is reality. Life begins and life ends. We cannot know when we will die, only that we will. Help us accept our mortality.

I have observed those close to death coming to full acceptance. There seems to be a point in time, Lord, when there is no other option, that people stop fighting the inevitable and embrace it. God, this is far easier to accept and believe when I know the dying person knows you. Your love casts out all fear. I know when my time comes you will see me through it and lovingly welcome me into your eternal home.

Help each of us accept death as part of life.

Thank you, Lord, for preparing a place for those who believe.

Amen

Day 69

Lord God,

Thank you for your help today. Thank you for seeing me through the commitment I dreaded carrying out. Thank you for soothing my emotions and helping me with my attitude. Thank you for giving me the ability to carry on. My arthritic hands were able to play the piano sufficiently. Thank you for your hand in my success. Thank you for friends who were praying for me. Thank you for seeing me through with your help.

Lord, thank you for the reminder of the angels you once sent to help me during a similar situation. I heard your voice bring that situation to mind and I knew you were with me. I envisioned angelic help around me. Thank you for their presence.

The obligation is now a thing of the past. It is behind me. The burden has lifted. I am free from it and need never agree to such again. I feel released, Lord, and may I remain so. I pray for future guidance in my answers of "yes" or "no".

Lead me, Lord.

Amen

Day 70

Father God,

I pray today that you lift the spirits of so many I know who are drowning in emotional baggage. Lord, free them. Free them from the continual trappings of sorrow and grief. Free them from constant worry and fear. Free them from perpetual anxiety and depression. Free them from guilt and regret. Free them, Lord, with your grace and healing.

Father God, I pray that each person will seek you. When we seek you, we find you, and our life changes for the better. I pray for the unbeliever to find you and the believer to know you better.

I pray, Father, for myself. I want to seek you daily and know you more and more. I want to seek you and know your voice better and better. I want to know your day-by-day plans for me. I want wisdom to guide me all my days.

God Almighty, I want to know you more fully.

Amen

Day 71

Father God,

I met a mother today hurting over her wayward son. In the grocery aisle, of all places, I met a hurting mother who is walking the same path I once walked. My heart hurts for her, Lord. Thank you for bringing us together as I shopped, and she stocked shelves. Two mothers bonded and shared their stories over something as simple as buying cocoa powder.

Lord, my son made it out of the darkness and is free from addiction. Her son, only twenty-one, sits in prison. He will get out, but then what? There is nothing left the mother can do for her son. He must make his own choices and live his own life.

Father, I pray for this mother who wants freedom and clean living for her son. I pray you will fill her with hope for the future. I pray you will sustain her and give her joy in her days. If she doesn't know you, Lord, I pray our talk helps lead her to you.

Father, I pray for her wayward son who has caused such destruction in his young life. Give him freedom from addiction. Help him find purpose for his life beyond drugs and alcohol. Help him find you, Lord, and be cleansed.

I pray for this mother and son, Lord God.

Help them.

Amen

Day 72

Lord God,

We are a mess here on earth. If only we could understand everything you have told us in your word. Lord, there are far too many interpretations. There are too many beliefs, too many denominations, too many religions, too many differences of opinion. It's mind-boggling and overwhelming to hear it all.

Surely, Lord, there is one truth and none of us have fully found it. It's difficult to understand clearly outside of our upbringing, our personal filters, our experiences, outside of what teachers and preachers tell us. I'm troubled by all the differences.

Lord, you are the one true God - Jehovah. I believe this because of my experiences with you. I ask you to help me to know you more and understand the one truth better. I will search the scriptures on my own. Devotional readings are helpful, and preachers are helpful, but God, they do not take the place of you and your word.

Help me, Lord God, Father Almighty, to study your word for myself, to hear straight from you the truth. Tell me all you can tell me and help me to understand. Lord God, may you be my one clear voice in this chaotic world of many opinions.

Amen

Day 73

Father,

I am being pulled again to hide away and go silent, to indulge in days of solitude. This pull is sometimes overwhelming. There is so much constant talking in the world. Too many words—words saying this, that, anything, and everything.

As I write may these words ring true. May I share them with anyone who will read and not be judgmental of those who don't.

Lord God, for those who read my words, may they find value, help, or camaraderie in them. May they feel they received their money's worth. May they feel these words are not a waste of their time.

Almighty God, help me never write words that are utterly meaningless.

Amen

Day 74

Dear Lord,

I'm feeling rejuvenated. I took a step back and let the woes roll off my back. I expunged them from my mind. I turned inward, Lord, toward you and my own thoughts, away from the constant talk. Not everything is for everyone. I keep sorting out what is for me, so I won't succumb to what I should not.

Every day, Lord, I carefully plan my path, yet it is easy to be pulled toward new ideas and ways of doing things that are okay for some but not necessarily for me. You know what is best for me. I ask you again, Lord God, to direct my steps.

Father, I asked that you fill me with ideas and plans that fit me and your plan for me. I cannot be anyone other than who I am, so keep steering me, Lord, more and more into who you created me to be. Show me the best ways to express myself.

Lord, teach me the best ways to share my work. Teach me what others need. Teach me how to meet those needs through the work you've given me.

May my heart and mind be open to you.

Amen

Day 75

Lord God,

Thank you for answering my prayer and granting me escape from sickness. I had major tasks to do that were threatened by being ill. But you spared me, Lord. You kept me from being too ill to complete my work and you graciously gave me extra strength and resolve to get the job done.

Thank you, Father, for hearing me when I call. Thank you for delivering me from illness and keeping me from injury. Thank you for uplifting my spirit. Thank you for the encouragement finishing the job has given me. Thank you for the boost of energy to help me.

Father God, thank you for seeing me through the work. Thank you for caring about our earthly situations and coming to us in our need. I recognize your presence, Lord. I know you are near.

Thank you for coming to me when I call.

Amen

Day 76

God Almighty,

I pray for all those suffering physical illness and injury today. I pray for a woman who's just experienced a heart attack. I pray for a young man terribly burned over a large portion of his body. I pray for a young child diagnosed with an inoperable brain tumor. I pray for another who received a cancer diagnoses.

Lord, I pray for those healing from broken bones and torn ligaments. I pray for those undergoing knee and hip replacement surgeries, and hand and foot surgeries. I pray for those receiving eye surgery or treatments to prevent blindness.

Father, I thank you and pray or the doctors tending each of these patients. May you give them great knowledge and wisdom. May you guide their skilled hands. May their work bring hope and healing.

Lord God, help us in our infirmities. We are at your mercy.

Amen

Day 77

Lord,

Thank you for my peaceful home. It is a haven of rest. Our home is a joyous respite. Thank you for the simplicity of our house and providing all we need. There is nothing else necessary than what we have.

We are grateful for air conditioning units and for our furnace. We live in comfort in every season. We have shelter from every storm. We do not fear.

Father, we have plenty of food and strong shelter. Thank you for our bed where we can comfortably sleep and clothes to keep us cool or warm.

Father, though we may sometimes replace furniture or add on to what we have, we know we have all we need already.

Thank you for your provision.

Amen

Day 78

Lord God Almighty.

We sometimes cry out in anguish. We cry from loss and grief, from frustration and lack. We cry out in pain and confusion and so much more. We cry out on behalf of another's struggle. We need you, Lord, to calm us and rejuvenate us.

Lord, as a man you experienced all we do. You experienced loss and grief, sadness and sorrow, hunger and thirst, being alone and misunderstood, weariness and temptation, frustration and anger. Lord, you experienced betrayal, ridicule, injury, pain, and slow death. Lord, you have cried, and cried for us.

Father, I believe you know my every emotion. I believe you know my every pain, every sorrow, and every joy. I believe you know my every capability, and my frailties. I believe above all that you know my heart. Knowing you understand everything about me soothes me, Lord.

Thank you for knowing and understanding me. You are all I need.

Amen

Day 79

Father God,

It is you who can change our circumstances or help us rise above them. You help us live above our struggles, not below them. You help us find joy even in our trials. Lord, the world is full of trouble and strife. Our only way out is to have your long reaching, strong arms to lift us up.

Father, you are the light at the end of the tunnel. You are the promise of better times. You are the hope that keeps us trekking forward. You are the ultimate caregiver. You are the healer of body, mind, and spirit.

Lord God, it is you who frees us from bondage of all kinds. It is you who understands our hearts and our psyche. Our past and our present. It is you Lord Jehovah, who knows every cell of our bodies.

I praise you, Father God, for your all-knowing power. It is a wondrous thing.

Amen

Day 80

Lord,

I was challenged today about my faith. I felt attacked. I know full-well what I believe and why, yet some will not let me speak it without further attack. I don't expect all people to believe exactly alike, Lord, but it would be nice if when I am asked a question, I would be allowed to give my answer.

God, not all people draw the same conclusions from your word, but I know you will teach any of us who seek you the truths you want to reveal. Help me hear your voice and your truths. Help me share with others what you wish me to share.

Lord God, I know my own experiences with you. I can share what I've experienced in my own life. It might help another, just as I learn from what others share. No matter our various experiences and opinions, help us all share the truths we've learned.

Amen

Day 81

Creator God,

It is a wonderful thing to have the love of a cat or dog…or any animal. Our dog is now with you, or wherever you have dog souls go. Our kitty is snuggling up against me as I write. She is affectionate and seeks my presence and attention. She desires me as I desire her—her soft fur so pleasant to touch and soothing to stroke. Petting her does us both good.

Father, it is beyond amazing how two very different species can live together in harmony. These little creatures living in our homes depend on us, Lord. We feed them and care for them and love them, showering them with affection. They thrive.

These animals, Father, give back to us. They seek our attention and affection, give us unconditional love, and let us love them. We need to love and care for others—people or pets. They seek the warmth of our bodies; their touch is beneficial to us.

The love between me and my pets has always been deep, Lord. It is wonderful to have them in my life and devastating when they die. Thank you for our loving cat. Thank you for her good health.

Thank you for these creatures who let us love them and who love us back so sweetly.

Amen

Day 82

Lord God,

What a wonderful, gentle storm you gave us this morning. Waking to the sound of rain on the windows and roof was so very pleasant. It was comforting and our bed felt extra cozy. Thank you for that morning greeting.

I thank you for bringing rain to our parched town. The rain was welcomed. Fall is arriving but still, the grasses are dry, and the plants desperately needed water. I had planned to water them today, but you did that for me, Father. I appreciate it.

The storm passed and the sun is shining. Nature is receiving all it needs today. The birds and squirrels have come to their feeders. It makes me feel joyful, Lord, to watch them thrive. Soon they will be tucked away during winter cold and snow, just as plants and insects will sleep and return next spring. Watch over your creation.

The steady changing of the seasons is fascinating to me, God.

May I always appreciate the magic around me.

Amen

Day 83

Father,

I feel small. In this great big world, I am but a speck. From universe, to galaxy, to solar system, to earth, to continent, to country, to state, to town, to neighborhood, to street, to yard and house, I grow smaller and smaller.

Yet, Lord, I do not feel insignificant. I have purpose and value within the time and space you have placed me. The century in which I live is far different from that of the people who lived so many decades and centuries before me. We are all tiny players throughout time, yet Lord, I feel I have significance.

My value and significance come from you, Father God. You have created each one of us in your image. To be like you in any way is magnificent and humbling. You have created each one of us uniquely, which gives us each a special purpose. No two of us are alike nor can we do the same things the same way. You have gifted us for your specific purposes.

Lord God, thank you for the value and worth you find in me…one so small in the great scheme of time and space.

You have given me worth.

Amen

Day 84

Lord,

I am continually amazed at the workings of our bodics, and that they work at all. Our bodies are miraculously strong, yet fragile at the same time. We are so easily susceptible to illness and injury.

I am grateful, God, that all the functions of my body are working properly, save a few old age issues that are not of much consequence. I know with further age I could acquire more difficult physical problems. I am constantly aware of the privilege to have a healthy body but know it could fail me. I do not take my health for granted.

Father, when I become sick, I realize how wonderful it is to feel well and I long for wellness again. Father, I ask you to keep my body strong, to keep me from harmful disease. I pray you will never let me forget how fortunate I am to be well.

Father God, I pray for those suffering ill health and ask you to place your loving and healing hands upon them. Bring miracles, Father.

In the miracles, we will praise you.

Amen

Day 85

God Almighty,

Another family has lost a son to addiction. That valley is deep and painful. Lord God, be present in their sorrow. Lift them high enough from the valley that they can see and feel the light of your love and healing. Sustain these parents, Lord. They are suffering.

Father God, I ask over and over, why do so many succumb to addiction? Why do they begin? Why do they continue? Why do so many not find the way out? Why Lord? Why?

I am one mother who did not have to experience the death of my addicted son. Father God, you answered my fervent prayers. You watched over my son. You saved him over and over. You helped him overcome his addictions and have saved his life and his soul. He found you and he found strength.

Lord God, I thank you and praise you for protecting my son. It could have been so much worse. I could have been dealt the devastating loss, as so many mothers have. I am endlessly grateful for his healing. I am endlessly grateful that you did not give up on him. I am endlessly grateful that the answer to my prayers was his release from addiction. Not death.

Lord God, some make it out and some do not. For the family who experienced the loss, and especially for the mother, Lord, I pray you wrap them in your loving arms and see them through this horrendously dark time.

Amen

Day 86

Father,

I need help with discernment. Sometimes a situation is clear but often it is not. I need help discerning peoples' requests. Some messages and requests are clearly SPAM. Others are true and real. Those in-between, Lord, are where I need help.

When do I stop and help and when it is unwise? I need to know. There are those, Lord God, who truly do need help, yet they are awkward socially or mentally ill. It is difficult to know how to respond to these people. There are many I categorize as "living on the outskirts of society". Their lives are more difficult. They don't quite fit in. They are often scorned. They are often in need. These people are often harmless, but there are others I am unsure of.

Father, don't let me turn a deaf ear or blind eye when someone truly needs help and I am able. Speak your voice of wisdom and guidance into my spirit. Let me know your will in each situation.

I seek your wisdom, Lord.

Amen

Day 87

Lord God,

It happened again. That trigger. That awful trigger that sends me plummeting into the emotional downward spiral of skepticism and fear. It sneaks up on me and latches its daggers of distrust into my psyche. This trigger, Lord, sneaks up silently then attacks viciously and throws me off balance.

Save me from these attacks, Father. You know my scars and tenderness. You know I truly have forgiven and have grown stronger and have handed this thorn to you long ago. It can no longer pull me into deep despair and worry as it once did, but Father, sudden attacks can still throw me off -balance momentarily.

But then, Father God, I remember I gave it all to you and you took it and saved me. You healed my shredded heart. You filled me with your spirit and helped me grow past the pain to a place where I am stronger and healed. Yet, Lord, my scars feel pricks of old pain at times. The trigger has not been fully removed. Maybe this is to remind me of who you are, how you came to me, how you nurtured and healed me, how I need only give it to you again, and to praise you for your help and healing.

Lord God, I need you. I call and you come to me and save me.

Amen

Day 88

Father God,

I met you before sunrise today. The cloudy, dark, dawn sky was spectacular. The quietness of the morning left opportunity for me to easily meet you. The distractions of the day had not yet begun. Morning is a powerful time of day.

It is afternoon, Lord, and I continue to feel your presence even in the activities of the day. My upstairs writing space feels sacred. The giant elm, outside my window, with its full, lush branches of leaves is awe-inspiring and pleasant to hear as it blows in the early fall breeze. Its leaves will soon turn yellow. The squirrels scampering across the limbs are entertaining and bring me pleasure with their antics.

Through the branches and leaves, I have a peek at the sky. It's blue and gray and white all at once. It is ever changing as the winds blow the clouds. Seasonal change is occurring. I enjoy the extraordinary power and the enchantment of nature as the seasons change.

Lord God, I enjoy and appreciate spring, summer, fall, and winter. I enjoy the day and the night.

Thank you for these gifts of nature and all they bring.

Amen

Day 89

Almighty God,

I am learning more and more just how near you are. It is I that sometimes moves away. Not you. When I get still and silent, I see you working and feel you close. All I must do it listen and seek to find you. It is in the quiet moments that I hear you the clearest. It is these still, quiet moments that I crave. I easily find you there.

I thank you, Father, for being so easy to find and approach. It never ceases to amaze me that while you're with me, you are also with everyone—answering their calls or calling them to you. You never stop working on our behalf.

At this very moment, a heart-broken mother is crying out to you. An abused or neglected child is needing you. An ailing old man or woman left alone is aching for your comfort. Confused teens and young adults are needing your clarity. Parents everywhere need your wisdom. At this moment an addict is ingesting, snuffing, or injecting a drug. An alcoholic is fighting the urge. A tiny newborn is fighting for its life. Another lies dying with his or her last breaths. In every case, Lord God Almighty, you are there ready to answer their call and need.

Lord God, may we all remember you are not far and are ready and wanting to answer our call.

Amen

Day 90

God Almighty.

I read a meaningful devotion on prayer this morning. The words of the writer reminded me of all that prayer is and can do. Prayer is powerful, God, because you are powerful. When we join with you in conversation and spirit mighty things can happen.

Lord, you can change horrible circumstances to good. You can stop evil forces that wish to harm us. Prayer is purposeful, intentional, and active. Prayer changes things, Lord, because we are asking you and engaging with you to use your power for good. In our troubles you can help. You can carry the weight of the world for us…as we cannot.

The pages of this book are prayers to you, Father God. Lifting myself and daily concerns and gratefulness to you. Meeting you in prayer daily is what I desire and seek. I long to meet you, speak to you, hear you, and know you.

Father, Lord God, Almighty may I never turn from seeking you.

Amen

"Give God your weakness, and he'll give you His strength"

-Anonymous

Dear Reader,

Thank you for reading this book.

May God richly bless you.

May his strength make you strong.

May he ease your burdens.

May he heal your sorrow and grief.

May he fill you with joy.

May he guide your path.

May you richly know him.

There is no better friend than God Almighty.

Amen.

Nancy

www.nancykuykendall.com

Made in United States
Troutdale, OR
04/08/2025

30452534R00076